Bible Stories Leader's Guide

for PreSchool Playground

Bible Stories Leader's Guide for PreSchool Playground is published by Standard Publishing, Cincinnati, Ohio. www.standardpub.com. Copyright © 2012 by Standard Publishing.

God's Backyard Bible Camp Team: Joe Boddy, Marcy Levering, Rosemary H. Mitchell, Becky Radtke, Standard Publishing Creative Services Team, Karen Statzer
All rights reserved. Printed in the United States of America.

Permission is granted to the original purchaser of this material to reproduce this book for ministry purposes only—not for resale. While Standard Publishing grants permission to alter and adapt God's Backyard Bible Camp, Standard Publishing claims no liability or responsibility for the content of any such adaptations.

Cincinnati, Ohio

BIBLE STORIES
Leader's Guide for PreSchool Playground

Using This Book 3
Resources Available 4
Decorating PreSchool Playground 7
A Night at PreSchool Playground.......................... 8

SESSION 1 Serve Family! 9
Joseph forgave and fed his brothers.
Genesis 37, 45

SESSION 2 Serve Friends! 15
Jesus washed the feet of His disciples.
John 13:1-17

SESSION 3 Serve Neighbors! 21
Rebekah showed kindness to Abraham's
servant. Genesis 24:1-27

SESSION 4 Serve Community! 27
Gideon led God's people in battle.
Judges 6:1-16; 7:9-21

SESSION 5 Serve Jesus! 33
Paul told about Jesus wherever he went.
Acts 27, 28

Age-Level Characteristics of Preschoolers 39

Using This Book

This book is designed to be a guide to help you teach preschoolers—make it work for you!

If your only job is to tell the Bible story, this guide, plus the suggested resources will be just about everything you need!

- The **Life Focus** is the main idea that preschoolers will learn and remember.
- The **Bible Memory** lists the passage kids will learn. Use all of it or a portion that is age-appropriate for your children.
- The **Bible Background** helps to prepare the heart and mind of the leader.

INTRODUCE THE BIBLE STORY:
Introduce the children to one aspect of the Bible story and the It's Your Serve! focus for the day. Words in bold face are suggested words for the teacher to say.

INTERACTIVE BIBLE STORY:
Let the children see the Scripture passage in your Bible and help them come to understand that the story comes from God's Word. The Bible story is written in regular type and directions for the teacher are written in italics.

IT'S YOUR SERVE: Apply the story to the children's lives and provide the opportunity for them to commit to age-appropriate acts of service in response to what they've learned that day.

If you are in charge of snacks, games, puppet skits, crafts, and service projects for preschoolers, you will also need the *Activities & More Leader's Cards for Pre-School Playground.* Ask your VBS director for these cards.

3

Activities & More Leader's Cards

The *Activities & More Leader's Cards for PreSchool Playground* are an important part of the PreSchool Playground program. They provide age-appropriate activities for the following sites or classrooms:
- puppet skits
- snacks and games
- crafts
- service projects

If you are in charge of all the activities for your preschoolers, use the activity cards to help you with the snacks, games, crafts, service projects, and puppet skits for the children.

These cards include great ideas and suggestions. And they also include directions, materials and supply lists, as well as review and application questions to help kids apply the activities to ways they can serve others! A complete list of supplies that are needed for these activities can be found on the PreSchool CD in the PreSchool Director folder.

More information about these cards can be found in the PreSchool Director folder on the PreSchool CD, which is in the *Age-Level Resources Disc Set*. You will also find complete PDFs of these cards in the same folder in case you need to print out more cards.

PreSchool Student Books

Bring it all together with a student book designed just for preschoolers! This full-color resource will grab kids' attention and draw them into fun activities and Bible reviews. Filled with a variety of learning tools, this hands-on activity book will help you make relevant connections in the lives of young children.

Here's What You'll Find:
- fun, interactive Bible reviews
- engaging application activities
- fun characters
- large community mural
- colorful stickers

This book will be a tremendous resource for you as you reach and teach kids for God.

SEND THE MESSAGE HOME!

At the end of every session, kids will choose an age-appropriate specific way to serve based on the life focus of the day. Write each kid's choice on a large address label. Each kid will peel off the label and add it to his shirt as a reminder of what he plans to do when he gets home.

More Resources

PRESCHOOL CD

Don't miss these valuable resources available on the PreSchool CD found in the *Age-Level Resources Disc Set* in the *SuperSimple*™ VBS Kit. They are designed to expand and enhance your daily sessions.

- Bible Memory Games and Rhythm—any or all sessions
- Bible Posters—one poster per session
- Coloring Pages—one page per session
- Serving Suggestions—sessions 1 and 4
- Puzzles—one puzzle per session

IT'S YOUR SERVE! STICKERS

Use the *It's Your Serve! Stickers* (025500213) as rewards, as reminders for kids to serve when you put them on papers that go home, for special projects, and more!

BOOKS AVAILABLE FROM STANDARD PUBLISHING

- *The House in the Middle of Town* (04737) teaches preschoolers about serving and helping their neighbors.
- *The Boy on the Yellow Bus* (021523010) will help preschoolers learn about being kind to others.
- *Surprise Bible Storybook* (025472811) introduces preschoolers to God, His story, and His Son.

SUGGESTED HAPPY DAY® BOOKS

- *Gideon, Blow Your* Horn (55000)
- *Paul's Great Adventures* (38008)
- *God Was with Joseph* (025487112)

Decorating PreSchool Playground

Decorating your room can be as super simple as putting up some of these colorful posters and decorations from Standard Publishing.

- Posters: *Bible Story Poster Pack* (025502413), *Site Names Poster Pack* (025499313), and *It's Your Serve! Poster Pack* (025499213)
- Wall or stand-up decorations: Cut out the art found in the *Decorating Pack & Guide* (025498813) and mount on card stock or foam core, or attach them directly to your walls.

LEADER TIP

You can iron the posters with a warm iron to take out most of the creases! They'll look great and mount much easier to cardboard or foam board!

Add your own special touches by looking in your own backyard or asking your neighbors for these items:
- any outdoor toys for preschoolers
- lanterns or holiday lights
- outdoor lawn chairs
- potted plants
- sleeping bags
- pop-up tents
- wagons

Look around at neighborhood yards, then come up with your own ideas for decorations!

A Night at PreSchool Playground

Spending time with preschoolers can be one of the most rewarding jobs you will ever have. Follow these steps to make it a great experience:
- Prepare and plan.
- Read and think about the age-level characteristics found on page 39.
- Have a backup plan ready for any emergency.
- Use all of the resources available to you.
- Remember, these materials are only a guide to help you.
- Enjoy your time with the children! If you think something won't work for your group of kids, adjust it so it does!

HERE'S HOW A NIGHT IN PRESCHOOL PLAYGROUND WORKS:

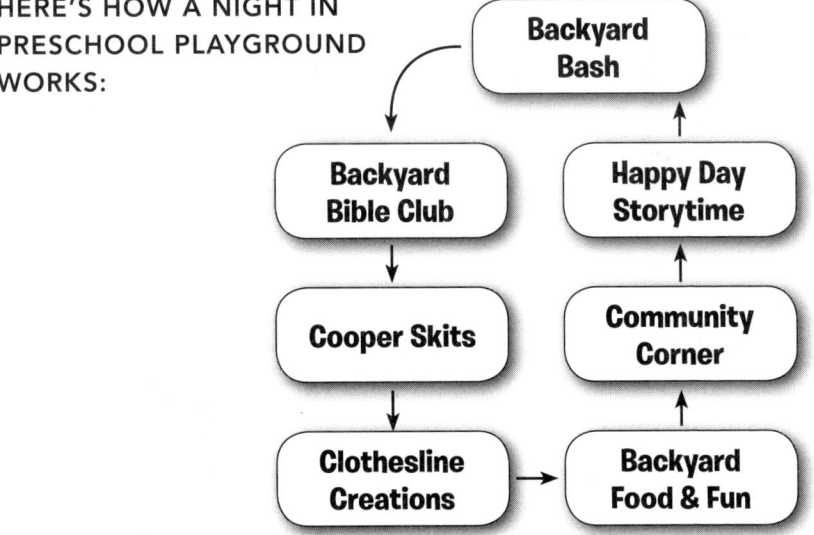

TIPS FOR TEACHERS
- You might want to make the *PreSchool Student Book* a separate site because of children's short attention spans.
- Add a Backyard Book site and read the suggested books (see page 6).
- Add a Bible Memory site and use the files on the Preschool CD to help children learn their verses.
- Add some guided free-play time (see the games activity cards for ideas) because preschoolers need time to interact with each other.
- Don't forget to build in time for restroom breaks!

SESSION 1

LIFE FOCUS Serve Family!

BIBLE STORY Joseph forgave and fed his brothers. (Genesis 37, 45)

BIBLE MEMORY Mark 12:29-31

BIBLE BACKGROUND

Jacob and his twin brother Esau were born to Isaac and Rebekah. Like Abraham and Isaac, God promised Jacob that a great nation would come from him. God blessed Jacob with 12 sons.

In Bible times, God did not regularly speak to people in dreams, but He chose to speak to Joseph through two dreams. The dreams indicated that Joseph would rule over his brothers and family, which made his brothers hate him even more. Reuben, Jacob's oldest son, planned to save Joseph. But instead, Joseph's brothers sold him into slavery, and Joseph ended up in Egypt. Through circumstances that only God could orchestrate, Joseph would become the second most powerful man in Egypt.

After more than 20 years, Joseph was reunited with his brothers. The brothers probably feared imprisonment or torture for what they had done, but Joseph realized that God had been in control all along. Joseph served his family by providing the food and forgiveness they needed.

THE DAILY PLAN

- **Introduce the Bible story.**
- **Involve the kids in telling the interactive Bible story.**
- **Apply the idea of serving to their lives.**

SESSION 1

SERVE FAMILY!

Introduce the Bible Story

Have your children line up in one long row. **Let's pretend we're riding our bikes around the block. We'll take turns stopping in front of everyone's house.** Walk around the room pretending to riding your bikes while you sing, "The wheels on the bus go round and round, round and round, round and round. The wheels on the bus go round and round, stopping at my house." Then turn to the line of kids and describe your house briefly and then name the people who live there. **I live with (name family members). These are the people in my family.**

Next, invite a child to be the leader and sing the song again, this time stopping at a different spot where he describes his house and family. Continue until every child has had a turn.

Did you know that God wants us to help our families any way we can? When we help our families, that's the same as serving them! Our Bible story today is about a man who helped his family, even when they weren't very nice to him.

COMMUNITY POSTER OPTIONAL ACTIVITY

Remove the covers from the *PreSchool Student Books* and give a community poster from the inside front cover to each child. Help the children:
- color the *Family* sign on the tree.
- circle their favorite backyard activities.
- put the Cooper sticker in the backyard.
- draw a family member next to Cooper.

As they work, ask them how they could serve that family member. Be sure to offer suggestions.

SUPERSIMPLE FUN!

Use PreSchool CD Session 1 Joseph Forgives His Brothers Coloring Page to enhance your teaching time.

SESSION 1

Joseph Forgave and Fed His Brothers

INTERACTIVE BIBLE STORY

Supplies: PreSchool CD Session 1 Joseph Forgave His Brothers poster, Bible

Have your Bible open to Genesis 45 to help the children understand that the story comes from the Bible. **Our story is about a boy named Joseph. During this story I'll stop and ask if you think what was happening in Joseph's life was good, bad, or so-so. If you think it's good, stand up and reach for the sky. If you think it's bad, crouch down low to the ground. If you think it's so-so, somewhere in the middle, then just stand up.** TIP: The expression in your voice will give preschoolers clues what actions to take.

Joseph was a young man and he had 11 brothers. They lived in a tent—much bigger than the ones we use to go camping. Joseph was his father's favorite son. **High, low, or so-so?** Joseph's 11 brothers knew that their dad loved Joseph best, and it made them jealous. In fact, they hated Joseph. **High, low, or so-so?**

One night, as Joseph was lying in his tent, he dreamed that he and his brothers were working in the field. His bundle of grain stood up tall and straight, but his brothers' bundles all bowed down around his. Another night, Joseph dreamed that the sun and moon and 11 stars bowed down to him. Joseph didn't understand yet, but God was using these dreams to tell Joseph that he would be very powerful some day. **High, low, or so-so?**

When Joseph told his brothers about the dreams, they hated him even more! So, they decided to kill Joseph. **High, low, or so-so?** But instead of killing him, they ended up selling him as a slave. **High, low, or so-so?** The brothers lied and told their father that a wild animal had eaten Joseph. And they thought they would never see Joseph again!

11

But many, many years later, a famine came to their land. A famine means there's not enough for everyone to eat. Joseph's family was running out of food! **High, low, or so-so?**

Meanwhile, Joseph was doing great! God worked things out so that Joseph now worked for Pharaoh, the king of Egypt! Joseph was a very powerful man just like in his dreams! **High, low, or so-so?**

And there was lots of food in the palace! It was Joseph's job to sell that food to people who needed it. It was up to him to give it out fairly so it would last a long time. One day, Joseph's brothers came to Egypt to buy food. They bowed down to Joseph—just like in Joseph's dreams—but his brothers didn't recognize him. But Joseph recognized them! **High, low, or so-so?**

Joseph had a choice to make. He was a powerful man and could have them killed or he could forgive them and try to help them.

Joseph realized that God had a plan all along! God used the awful things in Joseph's life in order to bring about something wonderful. Instead of getting even, Joseph forgave his brothers and then helped his family. **High, low, or so-so?** They all came to live in Egypt, and Joseph gave them jobs, land, and food. Joseph chose to serve his family!

REVIEW QUESTIONS

Use these questions to help the children remember the story.
- **Why did Joseph's brothers hate him?**
- **What did Joseph's brothers do to him?**
- **Where did the brothers go when they needed food?**
- **How did Joseph serve his family?**

BIBLE MEMORY

After reviewing the Bible story, use the Bible Memory Rhythm printable file with Track 1 or one of the Bible Memory Game activities, all found on the Pre-School CD, to teach the Bible Memory. The children will love how fun and easy it is to memorize Scripture.

SESSION 1

SERVE FAMILY!  It's Your Serve!

Supplies: copies of Pre-School CD Session 1 Serving Suggestions, sand bucket or pail, large address labels, marker, scrap mateial, glue, crayons, pencils

Before class, make copies of the Serving Suggestions. Cut them apart and put them in a bucket.

Gather the children in a circle. **Let's play a game that will help us think of ways to serve our families. See if you can guess what I'm doing.** Pretend to pick up toys. If the children have trouble guessing your action, give them some clues. **I see a lot of toys on the floor.** Once the children have guessed correctly, ask them to do the action too. **You can serve your family by picking up your toys.**

Quietly read one of the suggestions below to the child and have him perform the action. Encourage the group to guess each of the actions and then act them out on their own. **You can serve your family in many different ways.**

Setting the table	Putting toys away
Putting shoes away	Feeding a pet
Folding clothes	Raking
Planting flowers	Praying
Putting away groceries	Taking a bath
Drying dishes	Taking out trash
Dusting	Sweeping

13

SEND THE MESSAGE HOME!

Ask each child to choose a specific way to serve his family, then write his choice on a large address label. Have him peel off the label and apply it to his shirt as a reminder of the commitment he made. NOTE: Do not put labels on children's skin. Some children may be allergic to the adhesive, plus pulling the label off may hurt.

PRESCHOOL STUDENT BOOKS

The Bible story time is a great time to use the student books, but the children's attention spans may need a break. You can add a PreSchool Student Book site to your preschool VBS and let the children work on their student books there, or you may want to do them at this time. Either way, the student books are a great way to help kids process the information in the story in different ways.

Page 5

As the children color and then glue fabric to their pages, you'll want to talk about ways Joseph served his family. Ask the children to take turns retelling the story to the person sitting beside them.

Page 6

To help children think about the people in their families and ways to serve them, read the short couplets, one at a time, and have kids check the appropriate boxes. After they complete their pages, talk with the kids about what they will do to serve their families when they get home.

SESSION 2

LIFE FOCUS Serve Friends!

BIBLE STORY Jesus washed the feet of His disciples. (John 13:1-17)

BIBLE MEMORY Mark 12:29-31

BIBLE BACKGROUND

The Passover was a Jewish festival in Jerusalem focused on remembering and celebrating God's deliverance of the Jewish people from slavery. The crowd gathered for the Passover welcomed Jesus as the king of Israel. But Jesus' disciples didn't understand who Jesus really is, even though they had seen Him perform great miracles. Today's event takes place following the triumphal entry.

The custom of the time was that most homes would provide water for guests to wash their own feet or would provide servants who would wash the feet of guests. Foot washing was necessary because streets were dusty, and people wore open sandals. Low-level servants washed feet, a task not done eagerly or with love. When Jesus took off His outer garment and tied a towel around His waist, He identified himself as a servant. Jesus lovingly performed the act of service as an *example* of how we should serve. As Jesus served, so should His servants.

THE DAILY PLAN
- **Introduce the Bible story.**
- **Involve the kids in telling the interactive Bible story.**
- **Apply the idea of serving to their lives.**

SESSION 2

SERVE FRIENDS!

Introduce the Bible Story

Have the children sit in a circle. **We are going to play a game that reminds us how special our friends are.** Invite a child to sit in the middle of the circle. **Let's sing a song about how special (child's name) is to us.** Sing the following song to the tune of "Where Is Thumbkin?"

> (Child's name) is special. (Child's name) is special.
> Yes, (he/she) is. Yes, (he/she) is.
> I can treat (him/her) kindly. I can help (him/her) gladly.
> Be (his/her) friend. Be (his/her) friend.

After everyone has had the opportunity to sit in the middle of the circle, have the group talk about how friends should treat each other. Have each child take a turn naming a way to serve a friend. After each turn, ask: **If this is a way to serve, clap your hands.** Then emphasize that it is important to call others by their names, to tell others how special they are, to be kind, and to be helpful. **We can serve our friends.**

COMMUNITY POSTER OPTIONAL ACTIVITY

Distribute the community posters and stickers and have kids do the following:
- Color the *Friends* sign.
- Add the gate sticker. Tell the children that this gate leads into the Friendship Garden and that the flowers in the garden name ways to serve friends.
- Color the flowers.

Read the words in the center of the flowers and ask the children to circle one or two flowers that represent a way they would like to serve their friends. Don't forget to remind the children that *helping* someone is the same as *serving* someone.

SUPERSIMPE FUN!

Use PreSchool CD Session 2 Jesus and His Friends Coloring Page to enhance your teaching time.

SESSION 2

 **SERVE FRIENDS!**

Jesus Washed the Feet of His Disciples

INTERACTIVE BIBLE STORY

Supplies: PreSchool CD Session 2 Jesus and His Friends poster, Bible, large bowls of water (1 per crew), washcloth, towel, baby wipes (one box per crew)

Before you begin the story, make sure each crew leader or helper has a package of baby wipes to use as you tell the story. Have kids sit together in crews or groups of four or five and have them remove their shoes and socks.

(Open your Bible to John 13 and place it on your lap.) **God's plan to save us included sending Jesus to earth to die for us, and Jesus willingly accepted that plan.**

One night when Jesus was having dinner with His closest friends, He wanted to show them how very much He loved them. Jesus got up and wrapped a towel around His waist. He poured a large bowl of water and knelt down. What do you think Jesus was going to do? *(Allow responses.)*

(Using a towel, washcloth, and bowl of water, lovingly wash and dry the feet of a child as you tell the story.) Jesus washed the feet of His friends. Jesus—the perfect Son of God—was washing the dirty, smelly, ugly feet of His friends! Not because He had to, but because He wanted to. Why do you think Jesus did this for His friends? *(Let kids respond.)*

(Have crew leaders wash the feet of the kids in their groups. If some children don't want to participate, that's okay.) How do you think Jesus' friends felt as they watched Jesus do this? *(confused, surprised, uncomfortable, etc.)* They probably felt the way you felt when your feet were washed—kind of shy. Jesus' friend, Peter, was especially uncomfortable.

When it was Peter's turn, at first he refused to let Jesus wash his feet. Peter didn't feel like he deserved to have Jesus wash his dirty feet. And Peter was right about that. He *didn't* deserve for Jesus to serve him this way.

Peter didn't understand that Jesus was showing them how we should treat other people. Jesus said that if Peter really loved Him, he would let Jesus wash his feet. Then Peter said, "Then wash my hands and head too!" It was like saying, "Take all of me, Jesus. Whatever You want!"

Jesus was showing the disciples what He wanted them to do—serve friends! He didn't mean for them to go around washing each other's feet all the time, but He wanted them to serve others any way they could, and put other people's needs before their own—like He had just done by washing their feet. And that's what Jesus wants us to do too!

REVIEW QUESTIONS

Use these questions to help the children remember the story.
- **What did Jesus do to show His friends how to serve?**
- **What did Peter say when Jesus washed his feet?**
- **How did you feel when we washed your feet today?**
- **What else could you do to show you are serving your friends?**

BIBLE MEMORY

After reviewing the Bible story, use the Bible Memory Rhythm printable file with Track 1 or one of the Bible Memory Game activities, all found on the Pre-School CD, to teach the Bible Memory. The children will love how fun and easy it is to memorize Scripture.

SESSION 2: SERVE FRIENDS! — It's Your Serve!

Supplies: adhesive bandage, stuffed animal, blanket, Bible, puzzle, game, can of food, tissue or handkerchief, water bottle, candy bar, any other items that can be used to help a friend, tote bag, crayons, pencils, large address labels, marker

Before class, put all of the items you have into the bag. Gather the children into a circle. **Have you ever helped a friend when she needed it?** Give some suggestions if children are hesitant to answer, then allow a minute or two for responses.

I'm going to hold up an item, and I want you to think of a way you could help a friend with that item. Show the items one at a time and let the children respond.

How did Jesus serve His friends in today's story? When you go home, how will you serve a friend before you come back? You will be doing what Jesus wants you to do when you serve your friends.

SEND THE MESSAGE HOME!

Ask each child to choose a specific way to serve her friends, then write her choice on a large address label. Have her peel off the label and apply it to her shirt as a reminder of the commitment she made. NOTE: Do not put labels on children's skin. Some children may be allergic to the adhesive, plus pulling the label off may hurt.

PRESCHOOL STUDENT BOOKS

Page 7

This page of the student book helps kids visualize the Bible story. Ask the following questions as they work.

- What did Jesus do to show He loved His friends?
- How did Peter feel about what Jesus did?
- How would it feel to have one of your friends wash your feet?
- How would it feel to wash the feet of one of your friends?

Page 8

Play a game of "I Spy" for a few minutes and then continue the game using the pictures on page 8. Take time to talk about each picture and how the child is serving someone. Then let the children add the stickers to the page as they name ways they can serve like that to someone.

Use the following questions to help children understand how they can serve their friends:

- Who gives us friends?
- How can we help or serve our friends?
- How do you think it makes God feel when we serve our friends?

SESSION 3

LIFE FOCUS Serve Neighbors!

BIBLE STORY Rebekah showed kindness to Abraham's servant. (Genesis 24:1-27)

BIBLE MEMORY Mark 12:29-31

BIBLE BACKGROUND

God promised Abraham that a great nation would come from him. In their old age, Abraham and Sarah had a son named Isaac. After Sarah died, Abraham knew it was time for Isaac to find a wife.

In Abraham's day, marriages were usually arranged by parents or perhaps by a trusted servant. So Abraham dispatched his chief servant to travel to Abraham's relatives to find a wife for Isaac, knowing that God would provide the right woman. When the servant arrived at his destination, he prayed, asking God for a sign. Part of the sign was that the right woman would offer water to him *and* all 10 of his camels. In a deep well, a pitcher tied to a rope was dipped into the well and pulled up when full. In a shallow well, since there were usually steps going down to the water, a pitcher was dipped into the well by hand. Either way, getting enough water for 10 camels would have been a lot of work!

THE DAILY PLAN

- **Introduce the Bible story.**
- **Involve the kids in telling the interactive Bible story.**
- **Apply the idea of serving to their lives.**

SESSION 3: SERVE NEIGHBORS! — Introduce the Bible Story

Supplies: pillowcase, small tissue box, toy, adhesive bandage, thermometer, small blanket, Bible, apple, flashlight, water bottle

Before class, place the supplies inside the pillowcase. Have children sit in a circle. **Sometimes our neighbors are hurting. Their bodies might hurt, or they may feel sad, lonely, or scared. I've hidden some things in this bag that will help us think of what people need when they hurt.**

Have a child pull out one of the items from the pillowcase. **You pulled out a blanket. Sometimes our neighbors are sad because they miss their family. You could help someone feel better by giving them a special blanket to hold.** Have the children continue pulling items, using the suggestions to connect the item to a need. Ask the children to name ways they hurt and what makes them feel better. After each situation, say, **The Bible tells us to love our neighbors.**

Connections: tissues—comforting someone who's sad; toy—playing with someone who's lonely; bandage—helping someone who's hurt; thermometer—taking care of someone who's sick; blanket—comforting someone who's lonely; Bible—sharing God's love; apple—sharing with someone who's hungry; flashlight—helping someone who is afraid; water bottle—giving water to someone who's thirsty.

COMMUNITY POSTER OPTIONAL ACTIVITY

Distribute the community posters and stickers and have kids do the following:
- Color the *Neighbors* sign.
- Place the numbered stickers on the poster and then tell what they represent.
- Choose one of those ways to serve someone when they go home.

SUPERSIMPLE FUN!

Use PreSchool CD Session 3 Rebekah Coloring Page to enhance your teaching time.

SESSION 3

 **Rebekah Showed Kindness to Abraham's Servant**

INTERACTIVE BIBLE STORY

Supplies: PreSchool CD Rebekah poster; small, partially inflated balloons; water jug; large plastic bowl; brown paper bags stuffed with newspaper (or other materials to make blocks or stones), then stacked to make a pretend well; Bible

Explain to the children that you are going to let them act out parts of the story as you tell it. Choose some children (up to 10) to pretend to be camels carrying heavy loads. Help those kids place the balloons inside the backs of their shirts for humps, then kneel down on all fours. Choose one child to be the servant. Choose one girl to be Rebekah and give her the water jug. Tell the kids you will cue them when to begin acting out what you say.

(Open your Bible to Genesis 24 and place it on your lap.) In Bible times, the fathers decided who their kids were going to marry. Abraham wanted his son to marry someone very special. And he wanted her to be from his own country where he used to live. So he prayed that God would help him find the right wife for Isaac. Then Abraham sent for one of his servants.

Abraham explained to his servant that he'd been praying for God to bring a wife for Isaac. And he put the servant in charge of finding her! The servant was probably pretty nervous to take on such a big job. But he packed up his camels and hit the road, heading back to the place where Abraham was from.

(Cue the servant to start leading the camels around the room.) The servant brought so many things with him that it took 10 camels to carry it all! It was a long journey. It was a hot journey too! When the servant and camels got to the town late one day, they stopped at a well to get a drink of water.

23

(Have the servant and the camels stop at the well.) In Bible times, people went to a well at evening time to get their water for the next day. *(Have Rebekah come to the well.)* The servant had his camels kneel down by the well *(kids do so)* and then he prayed. He wanted to be sure to choose the right wife. He asked God that if he asked a young woman for a drink of water and she offered to give water to him *and* his camels, then he would know that she was the one God had chosen.

Before the servant could even finish his prayer, Rebekah walked up to the well. The servant saw her and asked for a drink. She gave him a drink from her jug of water, and the servant waited to see what would happen next. *(Pause for a moment to build suspense.)* Then she offered to give water to the camels too!

This was the one! The girl that the servant and Abraham had both prayed for. Rebekah went back to the well over and over again to draw out enough water for all 10 of those tired camels to drink. *(Have the girl pretend to be watering the camels.)* Why do you think she did that? *(Allow responses.)* She was a good neighbor to Abraham's servant. In fact, she invited the servant to eat dinner and spend the night with her family!

The servant knew for sure that this was the young lady God had chosen to marry Isaac. The servant went home to meet Rebekah's family, then Rebekah and Isaac had a long and wonderful life together—all because she made the choice to serve her neighbors *and* their camels.

REVIEW QUESTIONS

Use these questions to help the children remember the story.
- **Did the servant live near Rebekah?**
- **What did Rebekah do that made her a good neighbor?**
- **Did God answer the servant's prayer?**
- **Does God want you to serve your neighbors?**

BIBLE MEMORY

After reviewing the Bible story, use the Bible Memory Rhythm printable file with Track 1 or one of the Bible Memory Game activities, all found on the Pre-School CD, to teach the Bible Memory. The children will love how fun and easy it is to memorize Scripture.

SESSION 3: SERVE NEIGHBORS!

It's Your Serve!

Supplies: tables, large address labels, marker, pencils, Cheerios® oat cereal, quarters

Divide the children into small groups and have each group sit underneath a table. **Let's pretend that you are sitting in your house. The children under the other tables are your neighbors.** Go to one of the tables and tell the children that their next-door neighbor has a lot of trash in their yard. **How can you serve your neighbors?** Invite all of the children who answer your question to walk over to the nearest table and pretend to pick up trash and then return to their table. **You can serve your neighbors.**

Move from table to table asking the children how they can serve, using the situations listed below. Allow the children, who describe a way, to act out their service. Make sure that every child has the opportunity to act. After each action, have the children say with you, **I can serve my neighbors.**

Situations: are sick, lost their cat, are hungry, fell down, are new and don't know anyone, have a new baby, don't have a swing set, have been mean to you, would like to have some flowers planted in their yard, have a broken tricycle, wouldn't play with you yesterday, have newspapers in their driveway, don't know Jesus, don't have many toys

SEND THE MESSAGE HOME!

Ask each child to name a specific way he will serve his neighbors. As he chooses a way to serve his neighbors, write his choice on a large address label. Have him peel off the label and apply it to his shirt as a reminder of the commitment he made. NOTE: Do not put labels on children's skin. Some children may be allergic to the adhesive, plus pulling the label off may hurt.

PRESCHOOL STUDENT BOOKS

Page 9

Distribute page 9 and have the kids look at the puzzle pieces. Point out to them that the picture inside those puzzle pieces can be found somewhere on the page. Instruct the children to draw a line from the puzzle piece picture to where the picture appears on the page. Let them talk about the picture as they work.

Page 10

Distribute student book page 10 and the corresponding stickers. Have kids add the stickers anywhere in the green space. Play the game as described on the page. If you do not have time to play, explain to the kids that they can take the game home and play it with a neighbor.

SESSION 4

LIFE FOCUS Serve Community!

BIBLE STORY Gideon led God's people in battle.
(Judges 6:1-16; 7:9-21)

BIBLE MEMORY Mark 12:29-31

BIBLE BACKGROUND

During one part of Israel's history, God used judges to rescue His people. The Israelites would do evil in God's eyes, God would allow them to be oppressed, then God would raise up judges to deliver them. Gideon was the fifth judge.

Gideon was threshing wheat in a winepress, which was often a pit or recessed place in a rock, to hide from the Midianites. The angel addressed Gideon as a mighty warrior, possibly as a prophecy of Gideon's future accomplishments. Gideon, a reluctant leader, tested God three times. Each time God provided a sign that He would be with Gideon, and that Gideon would be victorious. In the Midianite man's dream, the barley bread represented Gideon and the tent represented the Midianites. In response to the dream, Gideon worshipped God. The attack against the Midianites began in the "middle watch," approximately 10 p.m. The combination of darkness, strange noises, trumpet blasts, and flickering lights caused great confusion.

THE DAILY PLAN
- **Introduce the Bible story.**
- **Involve the kids in telling the interactive Bible story.**
- **Apply the idea of serving to their lives.**

27

SESSION 4

SERVE COMMUNITY!

Introduce the Bible Story

Supplies: construction paper, clear tape, paper towel or toilet paper tubes, yellow tissue paper

Today our Bible story is about a man named Gideon who used some unusual weapons to stop his country's enemy. God had Gideon use only torches and trumpets to stop the Midianites! Let's make weapons like he used so you can help tell his story. Explain that a torch did the same thing for Gideon that flashlights do for us, and a horn was usually the horn of an animal that people blew through to make sound.

Distribute one piece of construction paper to each child. Help children make a trumpet by rolling the paper into a tube and securing it with tape. Then give each child a tube and a sheet of tissue paper. Have kids stuff one end of the tissue into the end of the tube. **These look like some pretty odd weapons, don't they? You'll find out how Gideon stopped the Midianites with weapons similar to these.**

COMMUNITY POSTER OPTIONAL ACTIVITY

Distribute the community posters and corresponding stickers and have them do the following:
- Color the *Community* sign.
- Place the library sticker in the correct outline.
- Place the fire station and police station in the correct outlines.

As the children place the stickers on their posters, explain that a community is where a group of people live in the same area or go to the same church, or do the same things.

SUPERSIMPLE FUN!

Use PreSchool CD Session 4 Gideon Coloring Page to enhance your teaching time.

SESSION 4

Gideon Led God's People in Battle

INTERACTIVE BIBLE STORY

Supplies: PreSchool CD Session 4 Gideon poster, paper plate, marker

Before class, use the marker to draw a scared face on one side of a paper plate. When you are ready to tell the story, show kids the paper plate you've prepared. **When I hold up my plate, you are to pretend to be afraid.** Let the children practice. Open your Bible to Judges 6 and place it in your lap.

Today, we are going to learn about Gideon. He was an Israelite, and his people had a BIG problem! Their problem was the Midianites. *(Hold up plate.)* The Midianites stole their land, stole their crops, and stole their homes. *(Hold up plate.)* Gideon and the Israelites had to hide to avoid the Midianites. *(Hold up plate.)* So Gideon and the Israelites cried out to God for help.

One day while Gideon was hiding in the mountains *(hold up plate)*, God sent an angel to give him a message. The angel said, "God is with you, mighty warrior." But Gideon didn't feel very mighty. He was terrified. *(Hold up plate.)*

Gideon asked the angel, "If God is with us, why are all these bad things happening to us?" *(Hold up plate.)* The angel told Gideon that God had chosen him to lead his people and rescue them from the Midianites. *(Hold up plate.)* But Gideon said, "How am I supposed to do that? I'm not strong enough!" He wanted to help his people, but he was afraid he wouldn't be able to do it. *(Hold up plate.)* But the angel told him about God's plan.

Gideon knew he wasn't alone, and so he did what God said. He was still scared *(hold up plate)*, but he trusted God's plan. *(Put the plate away.)*

It was still nighttime, and Gideon told each of his men to carry his torch inside a clay jar to hide the fire. He also told each of his men to carry a trumpet. Then Gideon divided his army into three groups. *(Divide kids into three groups and have them stand on different sides of the room with their torches and trumpets.)* Gideon and his army surrounded the Midianite camp on three sides. He said, "Watch me, and do exactly what I do." The men listened and followed his commands. Remember, they didn't have any weapons for this battle—no swords, no spears, not even rocks—only trumpets *(hold up trumpet)* and torches *(hold up torch)*!

Gideon blew his trumpet, and so did his men! *(Have kids blow their trumpets.)* Then they all broke the clay jars. *(Have kids raise their torches.)* Their torches shone like a ring of fire around the Midianites. The Midianites panicked and started fighting each other and running away. And Gideon's army just stood there and watched! The Midianites were gone, and the Israelites were free—thanks to God's plan and to Gideon, who bravely made the choice to serve his community.

REVIEW QUESTIONS

Use these questions to help the children remember the story.
- **What did God want Gideon to do?**
- **What weapons did Gideon use?**
- **What did Gideon's army have to do in order to defeat the Midianites?**

BIBLE MEMORY

After reviewing the Bible story, use the Bible Memory Rhythm printable file with Track 1 or one of the Bible Memory Game activities, all found on the Pre-School CD, to teach the Bible Memory. The children will love how fun and easy it is to memorize Scripture.

SESSION 4

 It's Your Serve!

Supplies: PreSchool CD Folder 4 Serving Suggestions, scissors, tape, large address labels, marker, pencils, crayons

Before class, make copies of the Serving Suggestions onto a variety of colors of paper, and decide if you have time to let the children cut apart the strips or if you should do it for them.

Show the colorful strips to the children and read what they say. **These strips will help you remember ways you can serve your community when you leave today. Let's put them together so you can wear them home!**

Demonstrate how to make a paper chain with the strips and let the children wear them around their necks. As children work, review what a community is. **(Child's name), how will you serve your community today? Can you think of other ways to serve? Who else can name a way to serve?**

SEND THE MESSAGE HOME!

Ask each child to choose a specific way to serve her community, then write her choice on a large address label. Have her peel off the label and apply it to her shirt as a reminder of the commitment she made. NOTE: Do not put labels on children's skin. Some children may be allergic to the adhesive, plus pulling the label off may hurt.

PRESCHOOL STUDENT BOOKS

Page 11

Let the children find and place each sticker on the correct outline space on the page. As they are working, have them retell the story in their own words, letting one child start the story, then having another say the next part. Afterwards, ask the questions at the bottom of the page.

Page 12

Help each child write his name in the space provided. Begin reading the story, stopping at each picture and encouraging the children to name it. After you have finished, read the story again, pausing at each of the suggested ways to serve. Encourage the children to respond to the suggestion in an active way: clap your hands if you can serve by picking up trash; nod your head if you can serve your community by treating library books carefully, etc.

Then have the children draw themselves serving in their community.

SESSION 5

LIFE FOCUS Serve Jesus!

BIBLE STORY Paul told about Jesus wherever he went. (Acts 27, 28)

BIBLE MEMORY Mark 12:29-31

BIBLE BACKGROUND

Paul had been arrested after a disturbance in the temple. Although judged innocent, Paul appealed to Caesar. So Paul was sent by sea to Rome in order to see Caesar. Sea travel was the fastest way, but also very dangerous.

Paul was just another prisoner until a strong storm attacked the ship. Because an angel had spoken to Paul, he was able to tell everyone that no one would be harmed and all should eat. When the centurion followed Paul's instructions, God was clearly at work, leading Paul safely to Rome.

Through the many events that happened to Paul and others on the island, Paul's actions pointed people to God and His power. After arriving in Rome, Paul rented a home for two years. Although always under guard, Paul openly taught about Jesus and wrote to some of the churches he had established. He likely wrote the letters of Ephesians, Philippians, Colossians, and Philemon while living in custody. Paul used his imprisonment as yet another means of serving Jesus.

THE DAILY PLAN

- **Introduce the Bible story.**
- **Involve the kids in telling the interactive Bible story.**
- **Apply the idea of serving to their lives.**

SESSION 5 · SERVE JESUS!

Introduce the Bible Story

Have each crew or small group sit in a circle with a crew leader. **Have you ever had news that you just had to tell everyone?** We're going to play a game where you tell someone something, then that person tells the next person—all the way around the circle. Then the last person will shout out the news.

Play the game for several minutes, making sure that each child who wants to shout a message, gets a turn to do so. *Suggested phrases:* a storm is coming, my dog is lost, dinner is ready, it's time for worship to start, the car has a flat tire, we're going to the zoo, it's my birthday.

Our Bible story today tells us how Paul served Jesus by telling everyone that Jesus loves them. When we help or serve others, we show Jesus that we love Him!

COMMUNITY POSTER OPTIONAL ACTIVITY

Distribute the community posters and corresponding stickers and have them:
- Color the *Jesus* sign.
- Trace their hand on the tree.
- Circle one thing they will do to serve Jesus next week.
- If time permits, have them color their trees.

When we work together to serve our families, friends, neighbors, and communities, we are also serving Jesus. Pray with the children, asking God to help them serve Jesus.

SUPERSIMPLE FUN!

Use PreSchool Session 5 Paul Coloring Page to enhnce your teaching time.

34 God's BACKYARD BIBLE CAMP™

SESSION 5

SERVE JESUS!

Paul Told About Jesus Wherever He Went

INTERACTIVE BIBLE STORY

Supplies: blue tarp, brown cloth, classroom chairs, marker, poster board, lengths of rope, empty boxes, Bible (Optional: palm tree or potted grass)

Before class, lay down the tarp and put rows of chairs on it to represent a boat. Make a shore area using the brown cloth and make a sign that says *Shore*. Write *Food* on the boxes.

(Open your Bible to Acts 27 and place it in your lap.) Paul was a follower of Jesus. He talked about Jesus everywhere he went. In fact, Paul traveled all over the place just so he could tell people about Jesus. Sometimes Paul got into trouble because he talked about Jesus—and this was one of those times.

Paul was a prisoner on a ship going to Rome. The ship he was on—*this* ship—was full of prisoners! That's you! Guess I'd better chain you up so you don't escape. *(Give each row of kids a length of rope. Have them hold onto the rope with both hands, pretending to be shackled.)*

There! That's better. Now, Paul had a bad feeling about this trip from the beginning because there were lots of storms at sea this time of year. He tried to warn the captain, but nobody would listen to him. So, as they sailed, up came a storm—a storm as strong as a hurricane! *(Have kids rock back and forth and bob up and down.)* This went on for two weeks and everyone was giving up hope.

Then one night an angel came to Paul and told him that no one would die in this storm. So Paul told everyone to be brave and to trust God, because he knew everything would be all right. Paul was so sure that God would take care of them that he started to eat! When the rest of the men saw how calm Paul was, they all decided to eat. Then they took the leftover food and tossed it overboard to lighten the ship *(have kids toss out the boxes labeled* Food*)*, but that didn't help.

Soon the ship crashed and started ripping apart. The soldiers set the prisoners free and told everyone to swim ashore. *(Collect the rope shackles, and have kids jump over the sides of the ship and pretend to swim to shore. Pretend to look around.)* Looks pretty deserted here, but the island where Paul landed was full of people. And can you guess what Paul started doing? *(Let kids respond.)* You guessed it! He started right back in, telling people about Jesus.

Eventually, Paul made it to Rome and while he was there, Paul continued to talk about Jesus to anyone who would listen—even the guards who were watching him! The Bible says that Paul talked about Jesus from morning until evening. Some people were convinced that Jesus was God's Son; others weren't. But Paul was never discouraged. Paul loved Jesus so much that he told others about Him every chance he got. And we can do the same thing. Because the Bible tells us that when we serve others, we are also serving Jesus—just like Paul.

REVIEW QUESTIONS

Use these questions to help the children remember the story.
- **What did Paul do everywhere he went?**
- **Was it easy for him to do that?**
- **What happened to Paul because he told people about Jesus?**
- **What are some good things that happened to Paul because he loved and served Jesus?**

BIBLE MEMORY

After reviewing the Bible story, use the Bible Memory Rhythm printable file with Track 1 or one of the Bible Memory Game activities, all found on the Pre-School CD, to teach the Bible Memory. The children will learn to love memorizing Scripture.

SESSION 5 — SERVE JESUS!

It's Your Serve!

Supplies: red construction paper or felt, scissors, marker, large address labels, pencils, crayons, paper clips

Before class, cut a heart from construction paper for each child and write "Jesus Loves You" on it.

If weather permits, take the children outside. **When we serve others, we are showing Jesus we love Him.**

Give one heart to each child. Suggest an action for them to do, such as hopping, skipping, spinning, pretending to fly, jumping, touching heads. While they perform the action, sing all or part of "Jesus Loves Me." When you stop singing, encourage the children to hurry and find a partner. Once everyone has a partner, ask each child to tell his partner a way he can serve Jesus. Then the pair should exchange hearts. Continue by naming different actions and encouraging the children to find different partners. **When we serve others, we are showing Jesus that we love Him.**

SEND THE MESSAGE HOME!

Ask each child to choose a specific way to serve Jesus, then write his choice on a large address label. Have him peel off the label and add it to his shirt as a reminder of the commitment he made. NOTE: Do not put labels on children's skin. Some children may be allergic to the adhesive, plus pulling the label off may hurt.

PRESCHOOL STUDENT BOOKS

Page 13

Read the instructions to the children and encourage them to fill in the boxes as instructed on the page. As they finish their pages, have the children retell the Bible story.

Page 14

Help the children write their names on the line provided. Give them each a paper clip and a pencil. Have the children put the paper clip in the center of the square and put the point of the pencil in the clip. Show children how to spin the clip. Ask children who land on Serve Family to give you an example of how to serve their families. Spin again. Continue this way with all the sections of the square. Provide opportunities for each child to share a way to serve.

Say, **When you serve others, you are showing Jesus that you love Him.**

Age-Level Characteristics of Preschoolers

Understanding preschoolers and helping them grow in the knowledge of God is one of the most important jobs you will ever have. Know them, love them, and accept them and it will make a huge difference in their young lives.

Physically, preschool children
- can't sit still.
- need a lot of physical play space.
- are developing eye-hand coordination.

Intellectually, preschool children
- have unlimited questions.
- learn by experience and by using the five senses.
- think literally and do not understand abstracts.

Emotionally, preschool children
- are generally self-centered, but naturally loving.
- are determined and shouldn't be discouraged.
- have rapidly changing emotions.

Socially, preschool children
- imitate others, so good examples are important.
- are uninhibited and need protection.
- play side by side but not always in cooperation with others.

Spiritually, preschool children
- are learning God made and cares for the world and people.
- are learning that Jesus is their friend and God's Son.
- know the Bible is a special book about God and Jesus.
- understand that prayer is talking to God, and God listens to their prayers.

These tips are taken from *Tips for Teachers: Early Childhood*,
Copyright © 1995 Standard Publishing. Compiled by Peggy DaHarb.

The SuperSimple™ VBS
THEME CHART

THEME BIBLE MEMORY
MARK 12:29-31

SESSION 1

Serve Family
Joseph forgave and fed his brothers.
GENESIS 37, 45

SESSION 2
Serve Friends
Jesus washed the feet of His disciples.
JOHN 13:1-17

SESSION 3

Serve Neighbors
Rebekah showed kindness to Abraham's servant.
GENESIS 24:1-27

SESSION 4

Serve Community
Gideon led God's people in battle.
JUDGES 6:1-16; 7:9-21

SESSION 5

Serve Jesus
Paul told about Jesus wherever he went.
ACTS 27, 28

Standard PUBLISHING

www.vacationbibleschool.com